Have I Got a Story for You...

Have I Got a Story for You

A Collection of Life's Lessons

PATRICIA HOGLUND

thanks for being a great support to me — you are now a part of my story —

Bel -

Pat

iUniverse, Inc.
New York   Bloomington

Have I Got a Story for You
A Collection of Life's Lessons

iUniverse books may be ordered through booksellers or by contacting:

iUniverse
1663 Liberty Drive
Bloomington, IN 47403
www.iuniverse.com
1-800-Authors (1-800-288-4677)

ISBN: 978-0-595-44084-9 (pbk)
ISBN: 978-0-595-88407-0 (ebk)

Printed in the United States of America

To my wonderful husband, John
And our amazing children,
Britt, Maeve and Marc.
I love you with all that I am.

And

Atum O'Kane
Your vision and constant encouragement
Made this book possible.
Thank you from the bottom of my heart.

Contents

Who Do You Think You Are?

When I entered school it didn't take me too long to become aware that I had some serious deficiencies, or so I thought. I couldn't draw. I could color inside the lines wonderfully. But trying to draw anything that looked like something recognizable was beyond my reach. I noticed later on that writing was not going to be my strong suit either. I would turn in these papers and I'd get them back with big red marks and comments like: "Start over." The unspoken message I received from this was that if I had any idea of doing something significant with writing I should reconsider. Try dance! Another area where I had my deficiencies. These were the messages I held in my subconscious about writing, until mid-life when I was introduced to journal writing. It was perfect for me. I could write anything that came to mind and no one would read it or put red marks on it.

I was perfectly content with this process until one day I heard this loud inner prompt to write. But I was writing. Then, the prompting was to write not just for myself, but for other people. That was when my inner critic went into overdrive. The messages I heard were: Who do you think you are? What makes you think you can write anything of value? No one would think you have significant things to share. So, I'd agree and the voice would be quiet for awhile, until I'd hear another inner prompt to write. This sparing match went on in my psyche until one day when I was sharing this struggle with a friend. He asked me whose voice was it that was speaking to me as the critic. That was easy; the messages were from my childhood that said: Don't get too big for your britches. Don't get a big head. Who do you think you are? Don't be a showoff. I also heard my mother, who was a hilarious storyteller, frequently repeat, "I could write a book but who would read it?" That message got embedded as, "You can write but no one will read it."

The other question my friend asked was, "Who was the voice saying 'write'?" After some reflection, I realized that it was the voice of my soul yearning to express itself, and to assist me in discovering new dimensions of life through my writing. It was not to be quieted.

Then, thru a series of serendipitous events, I discovered the Women's Story Circle organization. The group is designed to assist women in writing their life stories. I attended their first national conference and met an amazing group of women. Some of them were published authors, but many were just like me: women who were interested in capturing their life experiences through memoir writing, but who had no experience in directed writing. The organization had developed the concept of women meeting in circles and writing via a collection of topics that would elicit memories of their lives. We were encouraged to take the Story Circle back to our communities and facilitate a circle for other women.

I began hosting story circles where, together, women could explore the power of story. Many of us found the process to be transforming as we reflected on the richness of our own experiences and were able to put them in the context of our evolving journey. One woman even said that joining the circle was the most important decision she had made. It certainly had become that for me, as the mutual writing and listening to each other's stories became the container for the prompt: *write*. Little by little, I quieted the inner critic and started to share my writing in a more public way. To my utter amazement, I found that some people liked what I had to share. Eventually, I was being encouraged not only to *write,* but to publish my work. This book is in response to that prompting and to my own leap of faith. My soul's urging to *write* has made all the difference.

The Assistant

I am a very detail-oriented person, as well as a great multitasker. These skills were first noticed by my father when I was a young girl and worked in the family business. He told me one day that I would make a great executive assistant. He didn't tell me that I would make a great executive. This must have made quite an impression because later in my life, I embraced many assistant roles. I became a wife, mother, volunteer, chauffeur, school event cookie baker, etc. But, then I took on the "Great Assistant" role when my husband and I opened our own business. The agreement we had was that he would do all the legal work, since he was an attorney, and I'd do everything else. I became the receptionist, bookkeeper, human resources manager, advertising and marketing director, facilities coordinator, file clerk, accounts manager, supply procurer, lunch fetcher, and "other work as required" person—anything that needed to be done in the running of a business. My biggest mistake in all this was that I not only did it well and liked it, but I made it look effortless.

When I decided to do something more serious with my writing, I saw that it was going to have a huge impact on my husband for me to retire much of my assisting role. I decided the best way to engage in a dialogue about this would be to take him out to eat, where we could have some privacy, and I could explain the implications of this adjustment in my priorities in a relaxed environment. Over lunch, I began to explain the need for me to refocus my time into my writing, and that I was not going to be as available in my assistant role as I had been. Since I knew this would have an impact on his expectations of me, I wanted to be sure he understood the ramifications, and I wanted to know that I would have his complete support. His listened very intently and said he totally understood and wanted me to know that he was completely supportive of my emerging endeavor. He then asked if there was anything else I felt I needed to share around his understanding of the situation. I was so touched by his enthusiasm and acceptance of my sharing that I realized all my concerns about his response were needless and that he was totally open to my vision for my next undertaking. I couldn't have felt more complete and satisfied about the conversation.

As we began to leave the table to pay the check, he turned to me and said, "Are you going to the store on your way home? I need some cans of tuna fish and I'd like you to get me the very small cans, rather than the big ones." I couldn't believe what I was hearing. I became so frustrated that I didn't know whether to kill him or just laugh. The stunned look on my face must have jolted him into realizing what he had just said and the two of us burst out laughing. That was when I was sure my resignation as the assistant had been accepted.

The Call

I was raised in a strict Irish Catholic family. My mother went to church every day and my father was a Knight of Columbus, and he led the rosary every Monday night as it was broadcast on the radio. My two older sisters were nuns. My parents sent all of us to Catholic school.

Periodically, the parish church would sponsor an event called Vocation Sunday or Vocation Week. During this time, they would have a guest priest come in and talk about vocations to either the priesthood or the sisterhood. The priest would usually expound on the blessings of a religious vocation and the call that went out from God to join the religious life. That was then followed by letting us know how important it was to answer the call, and how we often found ourselves resisting but we didn't want to say no to God. A scripture story would be told about a prophet who had been called to some great work, like Moses leading the people out of slavery or a tale of some other luminary. I would sit in church next to my best friend, Jane Donnelly, and listen to them go on about all of this. I would find myself squeezing my eyelids tightly together as the devout do, and praying ever so earnestly that God would call Jane and not me. After all, she would make a much better nun than I would. She was obviously more devout, quiet, and really got along with the nuns. Unlike me, who was loud and, some would say, obnoxious, and I had spent way too much time in convents to be enamored with the lifestyle.

From time to time, if I thought I wasn't getting through to God with my request, I would move my seat in Church, figuring that God wasn't sharp enough to find me should He want to point the big long finger of fate at me. The one that would figuratively say, "*You*! I want *you* to be a bride of Christ." I wasn't at all sure that I wanted to be a bride to begin with, and I most certainly did not want to be a bride of Christ.

Well, to my ultimate gratification I became the bride of John Hoglund, and Jane became a nun. God after all does answer prayers, no matter where you sit.

Time Flies

This morning I was cleaning off my desk, and for the 417th month in a row, I changed the month on the perpetual calendar that sits on my desk. Surprisingly, I noticed how very tarnished the sterling silver had become. Upon reflection, I actually couldn't remember having ever polished it. As I was taking it into the kitchen for a cleaning, I was reflecting on how I came to have this quite exquisite Tiffany jewel.

It was 1968 and I was sailing from New York Harbor on a cruise ship bound for the Caribbean. It was my first cruise ever and what a time I had. I recalled my shipboard romance with the ship's doctor. It was a whirlwind. He was handsome, romantic, and very Italian. He was a musician and a fabulous dancer, and he waltzed his way right into my heart. As part of the festivities on the cruise, there was a costume party and I came as a tube of Colgate toothpaste. Much to my delight, I won first place and the prize was a sterling silver perpetual calendar from Tiffany's. Nothing came of the romance once we were on land, and the calendar has gone mostly unnoticed and uncared about for all these years. It did, however, keep perfect account of the passing months and years, and has accompanied me through the passage of my life.

Alongside the calendar sits a brass divider that has two slots, one marked "Today" and the other marked "Soon." I don't recall if it was a gift or something I picked up along the way to help me get more organized. I do tend to have fits periodically where I know the answer to my life's challenges is to get organized. It's funny how that thought prevails rather than the one that says: "Do something, anything, just not the same old thing." So, I was struck by the continual presence of these reminders of my creativity, and prompted to do it today, or at the very least soon. Time is marching on.

Waz Up?

My son turned seventeen this summer and all sense of normalcy vacated our home. It began when we bought him a small truck to drive to school. He suddenly found his new mother. The car gives him everything I used to: companionship, sense of purpose, encouragement, increased self-esteem, value, responsibility, and focus. They are joined at the hip. He is totally enamored with and obsessed with his alter ego. This developing relationship has been fascinating to watch. His talent for mechanics have suddenly emerged. The boy who couldn't figure out how to run the dishwasher is removing the dashboard and installing light switches. He is removing the front seat so that he can install the "amp" that increases the decibels on the sound system so the neighbor a mile and a half away can hear it, whether they like it or not. And, he washes the car daily since a little sap from the tree it's parked under has fallen on the hood. Meanwhile, the health department has quarantined his room because they believe E. coli is mutating in the carpet.

One afternoon, my son called me outside to look at the latest in a series of alterations he had done to the car. This one was frightening. He showed me his new speakers, which when turned on looked like the pulsating heart at the Museum of Science. To think that he was going to have these speakers gyrating behind his back while he drove made me think his internal organs would be so rearranged by the thumping, that we would never be able to locate his spleen again.

Then, the phone rang. He ran to answer it because 90 percent of all incoming phone calls are for him. He didn't answer it with an efficient, "Hoglund residence," or with a more cordial, "Good afternoon," or even with curt, "Hello." No, we had the standard greeting, "Waz up?" Forty-five minutes later when he ended the conversation, I inquired who was on the phone. "Eric," was his annoyed response. "What did he have to say?" "Nothing!" It's mystifying to think that the forty-five minute response to, "Waz up?" was nothing.

The other day I received a message from a friend who said he was so impressed with my son. He found him so polite, helpful, and mature when he answered the phone. My chest was about to puff up with great pride until I remembered that this articulate boy wonder had never given me the message that someone called.

My friends have dealt with the conflict of the telephone use by getting a separate line for their teenagers. Not me. I refuse to have the communications with the outside world managed by an eleventh grade dictator. My answer to the dilemma was to get a second line for my personal business use. This turned out to be a fantasy. The same person who couldn't figure out how to plug in the vacuum attachments had learned within minutes how to have a conference call on my two-line phone with four of his friends, so that they could jointly try and figure out "Waz up?" The President of the United States needn't have summits in Geneva to gather all the world leaders.

He just needs to contact my son and all major powers could be networked together in minutes from my phone. They just better make sure they know "Waz up?"

It is better not to ask too many questions that require reflective answers because it is a source of irritation to both parties. For example, one day as he was on his way out the door I inquired where he was going. His response was, "Wherever the road leads me, Mom." I suppose my response was too quick and too curt when I said, "Do you think the road could lead you to a job?" This was construed as an abusive confrontation. He suggested such and threatened to report me to the child protective services for cruel and unusual treatment. I all too quickly replied that he should get them on the phone and after I told my side, we'd see who needed protection. It went downhill from there. I've since given up the smart quip. It doesn't work. Locking them in their room is more effective, but the banging can be unnerving.

This all leads me to sitting at the kitchen counter wondering where I went wrong. I thought I did all the right things: helping out at school, reading bedtime stories, baking cookies for the birthday celebration at school, attending school open houses, and attending football games. Yet, it's all lead to a car-crazed, phone-obsessed, don't-talk-to me-I'm-going-out stranger, who has taken over my child's body and I'll never make contact with my sweet, precious boy again. Or, I could be wrong and he may be right when I ask him, "Marc, why do you behave this way?" He nonchalantly says, "I'm a teenager, Mom. It's my responsibility."

Dinner In

Last night at the dinner table, I reminded my husband and son that I would be out of town next week and inquired as to whether or not there were any groceries that they would like me to get from the store. The two of them looked up at me with a stunned expression like two deer that had been caught in the headlights of an oncoming truck. Then, the panic set in. I could see the two of them scanning their brains trying to figure out how they would eat all week. Perhaps they should watch reruns of *Survivor* to learn how they could scavenge the neighborhood for eatables. Or they could try and remember chemistry class to recall how the body metabolizes stored fat and converts it into calories. They should have paid more attention.

Then, my son had the inspiration of a lifetime and said to me, "Mom, do you think you could make meals for us and store them in the freezer?" I almost told him that hunting season was open and deer were prey. But I refrained. He must have me confused with Martha Stewart who probably would not only have the food made and put it in the freezer, but the oven programmed for the week so that everything could be heated and served on time. When I suggested that I was not Nancy the Nanny, and I was sure they could figure it out, they decided to pool their resources. My husband said he could make the salad. This consists of buying bagged, pre-tossed greens, cutting open the package, and putting it in a bowl. He also knew how to cut up a tomato and put it on top, and then get the pre-mixed salad dressing out of the fridge. My son's contribution was a bit more sophisticated. He said he could cook things on the grill and flavor them with teriyaki sauce. Chicken I could see, but who has teriyaki hot dogs? I was also terrified for a moment thinking of him firing up the grill outside my back door. I hope he contains the fire to the barbeque and doesn't walk off to watch the ballgame as my house gets fired up along with the steaks.

In truth, I know this is all a fantasy and that they will be preparing dinner as fast as they can dial the nearest take out place. I, on the other hand, will be spending my week having gourmet meals prepared and served to me. But they're not the only ones who will be roughing it. I will have to bus my own dishes after every meal. But, we all have to make sacrifices.

What Should I Do?

I have young adult children who live across the country from me, so we are often talking on the phone with each other. The other day I received a call from my daughter and she was amplifying the many melodramas in her life. I had been here before so I decided to lean back in my chair and listen to the tortured rendition of life as she was currently living it. I heard how the roommate was a slob and so very inconsiderate of any of her concerns or priorities. Her boyfriend was an insensitive pig and she couldn't understand how she could ever have agreed to go out with him in the first place. Then, her teacher was very unappreciative of all her great gifts and was mean because she was asking her to do things that were way above her reach. And, of course, the job was abusive. She had to deal with all of these hostile customers who never thought to say thank you, and her boss was completely inconsiderate of her feelings. In the end, she thought she should quit her job and school and move to Europe.

I had been sitting back filing my nails while listening to this ranting and trying to say the occasionally supportive, "Yes I understand dear, that must be hard," or the poignantly placed, "Yes, I see". Or just the curt, "uh hun." Suddenly, as if from nowhere, I heard her say, "So, Mom, what do you think I should do?" Totally shocked, I lurched forward in my chair and had this surreal experience where it seemed the pause button had been pushed on the phone and our conversation went into suspended animation. I started to tell her, "Well, I don't know why you ever picked your roommate to begin with. I knew she and you wouldn't be compatible and I'd get her to move out as quickly as possible. And the boyfriend was a complete loser from the start. That was apparent to the uninitiated. What were you thinking when you took up with him? As for your teacher, find someone who will appreciate your genius and never challenge you around anything. After all, who better to know your skill than you? And that job has been the worst possible place you could have picked to work. I'd file a complaint with someone about how difficult you are having it. Quit your job and move to Europe? What a spectacular idea. Can I come?" After this fantasized ranting of mine, I snapped back into my sane mind, the pause button was cancelled, and I was heard to say, "Well, I don't know, dear. What do you think you should do?" She does, of course, have all the answers for her quest and my job is just to listen to the ravings while she navigates the vagaries of life. Or, as Gertrude Stein said, "There ain't no answer. There ain't going to be any answer. There never has been an answer. That's the answer."

Moving Out

Yesterday, my seventeen-year-old son related a conversation he had had with one of his friends the day before. He had called to tell Marc that he and six of his friends had decided that when they turned eighteen, they were going to move out of their parents' homes and rent an apartment and live together. They wanted my son to join them.

Initially, my heart leapt into my throat as I thought of my son and how young he was, how unprepared he would be for this kind of transition, and how I would want to convince him of an alternate plan like going away to school first. These moves always seem to facilitate the transition from home. I also quickly thought of how many life skills he hadn't mastered yet, like how to do the laundry, cook, clean, or shop, etc. I needn't have been concerned.

When I asked my son what he said in response to the invitation, he said, "I told him, 'Are you nuts? Why would I want to move out of my parents' home? The first thing I'd have to do is get a full-time job to buy my car from them, and then I'd have to pay for the insurance, gas, and upkeep. If I left, my mother would no longer do my laundry or cook for me. And I wouldn't have her around to pinch the odd twenty dollar bill for movies, and what would happen to my dog? They probably wouldn't let me take her with me. No way will I move out any time soon."

I sat there and listened to his response in stunned silence. At first, I was so pleased that he had an accurate assessment of how little he knew about setting up housekeeping. But, upon further reflection, I realized how much service I provided for "my baby" and how much money it really is costing me. Is it really appropriate for an eighteen-year-old, "emancipated youth" as my estate planning attorney keeps referring to him, to still be living the life of luxury at my expense? And come to think of it, why doesn't he have a job and why am I always giving him money for recreation? Then I thought, enough is enough. He should be out on his own making his own way. Perhaps I'll call his friend and say that if I can get Marc to move in with them, I'll contribute the dishes, pots and pans, and buy the first month's groceries. Emancipation comes at a price.

Uncle Charlie

$\mathcal{M}y$ Uncle Charlie and Aunt Anna used to take a trip to Florida every year for their vacation. This particular year they invited Anna's sister, Dolly, to join them. The night before they were to leave, Dolly came down to their house to stay so that they could get an early start.

After dinner, they sat around and visited as families often do, rehashing the latest events in each of their lives and telling stories of past excursions. Uncle Charlie was an "early to bed, early to rise" kind of guy, so after he had all he could handle of the re-telling of past adventures, he announced that he was going to bed and they should do the same because he wanted to get an early start. Dolly and Anna assured him that they would be right behind him in calling it a night. At 11:00 PM, Uncle Charlie woke and came out to the kitchen to find Dolly and Anna still chatting there. He once again encouraged them to get to bed as he wanted to get on the road early. Again, they assured him that they were coming to bed. At 1:00 AM, they finally thought they had better head to bed and get at least a few hours of sleep. At 2:00 AM, Charlie woke again and came out to the kitchen, but this time he couldn't go back to sleep so he decided he might as well get a very early start and proceeded to dress. When he finished, he went around the house and turned all the clocks ahead to 5:00 AM. Charlie then woke the sisters to tell them it was time to leave. They were completely dazed when he woke them. As they staggered to their feet and tried to navigate to the bathroom and get dressed, Anna said to Charlie that she felt like she had just gone to bed since she was so tired. Charlie's response was that he had told them to go to bed early and they should have taken his advice. After stumbling down to the car, they were off on the grand adventure. After several hours of riding in the car, Dolly finally said, "Charlie, don't you think it should be getting light pretty soon. It seems the sun should be up by now." Charlie had to fess up to what he had done. They were not amused, but the next year they were in bed early and ready to go when Charlie called.

The Long Good-bye

My son left for college today and after the teary good-bye in the driveway, I came back inside the house and went and sat in his room. It had been transformed from an active young adult man's room to what looked like a guest room. All of the pictures on the walls had been removed, the game box was gone, all of the letter shirts were taken down, and the collage of school pictures were packed away. It was so neat and tidy; it was hard to tell that the room had been jam-packed with all the trappings of an active, engaged student. As I sat there feeling quite disoriented, I was suddenly taken back to another room that I sat in that looked like a guest room. It was actually a guest room, but this room was about to be converted into a nursery. I was preparing for the arrival of my baby and much activity was involved. The crib had to be set up, the bassinet had to be borrowed from a friend, the changing table and rocking chair had to be put into place. The nursery rhyme pictures were hung on the wall and the comforters, diapers, and rattles were all neatly arranged in drawers; all in preparation for the new bundle of joy who would be arriving soon. Finally, the day arrived when I brought my newborn son home and we were both cozily enveloped in this haven we called a nursery. Now, as I sat with all the memories of the life we had shared during those intervening times, I realized that all those years before I had really prepared a room for him in my heart and that room would always be fully furnished.

The Music Plays On

There they are again, those feelings of disconnectedness—except the disconnectedness is not from a place or person or a feeling or an experience, but it is being disconnected from me. When was it that I first lost my way? When was it that I took that first step away from me that ultimately led to me abandoning me entirely? It didn't seem so critical in the beginning that I said no to me. How was it that I first started to quiet the still small voice inside of me? Was it when I came to the fork in the road and I knew my path went to the right, but everyone else said, "No, no one ever goes down there—come with us to the left and we'll show you the way and be your companion and point out the known guideposts," and I didn't stay long enough to protest. Or perhaps it was the first tiny insignificant pleasing thing to avoid censure or criticism or a hard look. It didn't seem important at the time. What harm is there in going along with someone else's vision? After all, that's what supportive people do, don't they? How was it that I managed to silence the symphony playing inside of me? It wasn't as if I only played bass, or the only sound

I heard periodically was a light tinkling on the triangle. Mostly, I heard the violins playing the melody, the score for my life. And didn't I always hear the bassoon with that rich deep resonance that one feels in the bottom of your feet? Or the tympani always keeping the beat and the horns calling me hither? It wouldn't have been possible to disconnect all at once just by the lowering of the baton. It must have been one instrument at a time until all the music was gone, and so was I. I wasn't abandoned along the way by a mad lover or a disappointment or a cold glance. I left me. One day at a time, one lie at a time, one compromise at a time. One "it really doesn't matter" at a time. How was it that I managed to abandon the one I loved more than anyone else? The "I" in the "I am." With whom did I think I could replace her and now how do I recover her? Is it in one violin at a time or one French horn or one bassoon? Or is it in the tinkling of a small bell and each time it rings I respond, "I am here and I love you and I will never leave you again"?

The Sunflower Lady

Some of life's lessons come to you in the most unexpected ways. This lesson happened when we took our children back to visit my family in New Jersey. My brother had made arrangements for us to spend the first night in a hotel and we would all meet up for dinner. After we were unpacked and settled into the room, I called him to decide where we would eat. His first question was, "What kind of food would you like?" Without hesitation I said, "Italian since there are few places to get really good southern Italian food where I live in Seattle." My only caveat was that I didn't want any place too fancy since we had all of our teenage children with us and needed to keep it fairly simple. He replied that he had just the place for us, told us how to get there, and we agreed to meet at 6:00 PM.

When we arrived at the restaurant, I immediately knew I was in trouble. It was not the low-key place I had asked for, and I should have protested, but thought I'd take a chance. We were shown to our table, which was elegantly set with linens, silver service, and enough glasses to sample several different beverages. The napkins were inside one of the glasses and

27

when the waiter approached the table, he removed the napkin from the glass, placed it on my lap, and asked, "Madame, what would she like to drink?" I don't know whether my brother ever saw the lightening-sharp glares I was sending his way about bringing us to this fancy place, but I'm sure my children knew from my telepathic glare that if they started a food fight they were dead. All of the sudden, the table of six next to us broke into rounds of "O Solo Mio." I felt like I was going to lose total control of this dining experience and that nothing else could possibly jar my nerves, when I saw her. My eye suddenly caught sight of this woman standing at the entrance to the restaurant. I thought I was looking at a sunflower incarnate. There she stood, dressed in a flowing smock made of printed sunflower material. She had a straw hat with the biggest sunflower I had ever seen attached to the front. Her drop earrings had huge sunflowers on them and her ring was also a sunflower. Her purse was a plastic see-through, but had giant sunflowers pasted all on the front. To finish off this most extraordinary outfit, she was wearing white ankle-length boots with, you guessed it, two magnificent sunflowers. She stood there in complete composure as she spoke to the maître d', who didn't seem to be a bit fazed by her presence. He appeared to be asking her if she wanted a table for two or if she would be dining alone. She, on the other hand, seemed to be saying, "I'll have a table by the window." While this perceived banter went on, I was speechless and completely transfixed. It was all I could do not to jump up from my seat, rush over to her, throw her to the floor, and remove all her clothes and put them on as quickly possible. Then, I would assume her position at the entrance to the restaurant, just for the brief experience of seeing the world through the persona of someone who was so totally self-contained, or so crazy that she managed to navigate the world on her terms and expected to be received accordingly. Before I could leave my seat, some distraction occurred at the table, perhaps my children were arguing over who got the bread basket next or why they hated anchovies. When I cast my momentarily-averted glance back to the door, she was gone. She never took her seat by the window, and never had a companion meet her. In those brief moments, she left an abiding memory for me to attempt to live out of my authentic self, even if it meant looking like a sunflower.

Shopping Nightmare

I hate grocery shopping. There is nothing creative or inspiring about it. You go to the store, fill up your cart, check out, bring it home, store it, cook it, they eat it, and you start all over again. No one in my family has ever been standing by the door when I come home from shopping and while helping unpack the groceries exclaimed, "Look! Mom found a perfectly round tomato at the store. Isn't she amazing?" No. They're not there at all. They never notice what condition the food is in, as long as it is eatable. So, I go to the store on a mission: get in and get out as fast as possible, with as few incidents as possible. I do not go to the store for an experience. Like the woman who made it to the celery just before I did today. She picked up at least five stalks of celery and carefully looked at them, then replaced each one and picked up another. I didn't get it. Celery is celery. Unless the tops are all curled, in which case you know it has been in the case way too long and you should find a better grade of store to shop at, celery is pretty much all the same. But somehow she felt there was the perfect stalk. I couldn't watch. I moved on to the mushrooms and came back.

I also do not want to be harassed in the store. Like the day I was looking for something which I couldn't find, so I asked the nearest clerk if he had the item. He looked at me in utter dismay, pulled himself up as tall as he could, and said, "Madame [I hate when they call me that, too], we wouldn't have that. It has preservatives in it." I looked at him as if to say, "And your point is?" I can't stock my home shelves full of stuff without preservatives because then I would have to come to the store more frequently and talk to more people like him. Anyway, I moved on to something fresh.

I also hate it when the store decides to rearrange all the aisles. Just when I have the store figured out and know where everything is (so I can get in and out even faster), some person, who obviously doesn't have enough to do, decides that they should redo the store. I know it must be someone who hates people like me and just wants to slow me down, so maybe I'll buy something new since I have never been down that aisle before.

When I finally get to the checkout line, I somehow always pick the one that has people with issues in it. Either they have picked an item that doesn't have a price on it and it is not in the database, and no one in the store knows the price, so they have to call corporate to see what to charge; the person has fifty-five coupons and the checker has to make sure every coupon has a corresponding item; or, the person finds when the total is rung that they don't have enough money, so they start returning things until they get to an amount they do have. Or, my favorite, the person paying by check who stands and patiently watches every item being scanned and then when they get the total, decide they will write a check and start pawing thru their purse looking for the checkbook etc., etc., etc.

Today, however, was the topper. I got into a checkout line where the checker must have been on drugs. He looked like he was operating in slow motion. He carefully picked up each item, looked at it, sort of juggled it, slowly ran it by the scanner, and then carefully put it on the counter. He was also having a running conversation with the woman customer, making some comment every time he picked up an item. She never said a word. Then, he pressed the total button and she started to write a check when, to his total amazement, he found a bag in the cart. He ever so slowly looked in it only to find it had doughnuts that he had failed to ring up and a bunch of flowers that he missed, too. After he rang those up, she had a new total, but she had already written the check. So, he asked her if she had a store card so maybe the discounts would bring the total under the amount she had written. She frantically rummaged in her purse for the card and he scanned it, only to find she had bought nothing on sale. He then told her she could just change the amount of cents on the check and initial it. After she did that, he noted that the dollar amount was wrong so she would have to fix that, too. By this time, she was so frustrated, she decided to write a new check; more rummaging in her purse. Finally, she got the check written, groceries bagged, and off she went. By this time, the guy in the aisle next to me (the one I didn't go in) had his three-hundred-dollar order priced, bagged, and paid for. By now, I was so crazy I wanted some of whatever the guy was on and wanted him to step aside so that I could scan my own order and get out before the sun set. I said nothing to him, bagged my own groceries, paid by cash, and fled, swearing my family could starve before I would do another day of grocery shopping.

The Next Step

My daughter graduated from college last month. A few days before graduation, I was clearing off my desk and her passport fell on the floor. As I picked it up, I realized that I was no longer the keeper of her passport, and then I thought of how I was no longer the keeper of her dreams. She has her own vision now and my job is to support her in discovering and living out her own dreams. Part of me is rejoicing in seeing her at the beginning of a new and thrilling life, but part of me wants her to wait, come home for the summer, and have one more round of special times together. There are few, if any, incompletes that I feel about our twenty-two years together, but it seems like it was such a short time. I suppose my fear is that she will have a busy life just like the one I've lived, and not find time to call her mother. It's not that she won't think of me or care about me or want to talk to me. It's just that so many other things will fill up her time. Not more important things, just equally as important things, like work, friends, a husband and children, houses, cell phones, e-mails, a social life, community work, and another world that I will never experience fully. And that's the way it should be, and the way I want it to be for her. I just didn't think we would get here so fast. Standing in the rain watching all the fast pitch games seemed like an interminable amount of time; every dance rehearsal and recital seemed stacked one on top of the other, endless. Every swimming lesson seemed like it went on for eternity, coupled with the ballet lessons, drill team contests, school events, prom, and birthday parties. I some how felt I'd be doing them forever. But now, I realize that her friends will be giving the birthday parties, just like they are helping her put together her apartment. Her friends are taking the pictures of the dances. Her friends get to meet the boyfriend first. I suppose there will be times that mom will be the number-one assist, at the wedding and the arrival of the babies, if any of that takes place. But for now, she is to be a fellow traveler on the journey of life. What a blessing it has been to have had her so close for this long and to think of all the wonderful moments we will get to share together in the future. It will just be different, different for both of us.

Place as Teacher

My goal after graduate school was to move to Seattle. I loved the big city. But the best-laid plans don't always turn out that way. I ended up in the state capitol, population-forty-six thousand. I was unhappy from the beginning. There was nothing of all the things I loved. No major theatre or symphony, no opera, and few, if any, nationally known public lecturers. The college was small and new. The population was too homogenous and although beautiful, the city was anything but cosmopolitan. The job opportunities were limited and I felt adrift in my new world.

There were pieces that I later discovered were very similar to my town of origin. It was small enough that you knew people when you went to the store. The merchants knew your name. You could have a personal relationship with the banker, the dry cleaner, and the fish seller, and it was easy to be involved in local affairs. All the things I was trying to get away from by being in a big city. I was looking for anonymity.

Regardless of all my complaints, I lived there for over thirty years. We raised our children there, had a very successful business, lived in a beautiful home on the waterfront, and made friends and participated in the community. Finally, after a series of events, we sold everything and moved to Seattle. I couldn't be happier. All of my fantasies about living in the city are coming true. I love my newly created life.

There has been one lingering question that haunts me: What was I doing in that small town, so unhappy, all those years? The answer came in a most unexpected way. I was attending the women's story circle conference in Texas and in one of the breakout sessions the facilitator had us write about a place. The instructions were to map all the places we had ever lived and then mark the one where we had lived the longest, and write about that place. So, I found myself writing about my thirty years in this small town and thinking about why I was there. On reflecting about how it was very familiar to me in its likeness to the town where I was raised, I realized that there was a certain amount of comfortableness about the place. On the other hand, since it didn't have any of the glitz that I wanted from a big city, I couldn't be continually engaged in all the distractions it had to offer. So, in the end, what I was left to do was change my inner landscape. I spent many years in therapy working on my old issues, I read a wealth of self-help books, I spent hours in group sessions dealing with past traumas, and I spent weeks in workshops learning how to live an authentic and transparent life. Only after all of this was I able to move to the "big city" and completely feel at home, not only in my outer landscape but with my inner landscape. The thirty years I thought I had wasted had, in fact, been the perfect place to nurture and grow my inner experiences so I now can live each day with gratitude and enthusiasm. Life seems to have a way of working out in the end.

Printed in the United States
128148LV00005B/4/P